AN IMAGINATION LIBRARY SERIES

WORLD'S LARGEST
SNAKES

Reticulated
Pythons

by Valerie J. Weber

Please visit our web site at: www.garethstevens.com
For a free color catalog describing Gareth Stevens Publishing's
list of high-quality books and multimedia programs,
call 1-800-542-2595 (USA) or 1-800-387-3178 (Canada).
Gareth Stevens Publishing's fax: (414) 332-3567.

Library of Congress Cataloging-in-Publication Data available upon request
from publisher. Fax (414) 336-0157 for the attention of the Publishing
Records Department.

ISBN 0-8368-3656-1

First published in 2003 by
Gareth Stevens Publishing
A World Almanac Education Group Company
330 West Olive Street, Suite 100
Milwaukee, WI 53212 USA

Text: Valerie J. Weber
Cover design and page layout: Scott M. Krall
Series editor: Jim Mezzanotte
Picture Researcher: Diane Laska-Swanke

Photo credits: Cover, p. 7 © Jack Milchanowski/Visuals Unlimited; p. 5 © Ingo Arndt/naturepl.com;
p. 9 © Chris Mattison; p. 11 © P. Morris/Ardea London Ltd.; p. 13 © Joe McDonald/Visuals
Unlimited; pp. 15, 19 © James E. Gerholdt; p. 17 © Elizabeth S. Burgess/Ardea London Ltd.;
p. 21 © Brian Kenney

Printed in the United States of America

1 2 3 4 5 6 7 8 9 07 06 05 04 03

Front cover: **This reticulated python is waiting
for a meal to pass by it. The snake's gleaming
eyes have no lids.**

TABLE OF CONTENTS

Words that appear in the glossary are printed in **boldface** type the first time they occur in the text.

The Longest, but Not the Biggest

The reticulated python is the longest snake in the world. It can grow to a length of almost 33 feet (10 meters). So why is the green anaconda, which grows to a length of about 30 feet (9 m), the world's biggest snake? The anaconda is thicker and weighs more than the skinnier reticulated python.

Reticulated pythons are found in the hot and humid lands of Southeast Asia and the Philippines, including the Australasian islands, such as Sulawesi in Indonesia. They are good swimmers, and they live near rivers and lakes as well as in forests, grassy areas, and **scrubland**.

The reticulated python uses the thick skin of its belly to help pull itself along tree limbs, pushing its skin into the bark to get a good grip.

How Do You Measure a Python?

It is hard to measure reticulated pythons. For a snake to be measured, it has to be straightened out, but a reticulated python is like a heavy steel **cable**. These snakes are so powerful, even several trained zookeepers cannot pull them straight! In zoos, a python is measured by running a string down its backbone and then measuring the string.

Even dead, a reticulated python is difficult to measure. Its skin overlaps in many folds. When the dead snake is stretched out, the folds straighten, making the snake appear longer than it really was when it was alive. The skin can stretch to as much as one-fourth longer than the size of the live snake.

The python's skin has overlapping folds that make it easy for the snake's entire body to get wider. A stretchy body allows room for some very big meals!

Colorful, Sparkling Scales

Reticulated pythons are silver to gray in color. They are covered with brown, gold, gray, olive, and tan splotches with black outlines. The reticulated python gets its name from this **network** of outlines. "Reticulated" means "covered with a network."

Scales cover nearly every part of a snake. These scales are made mostly of keratin, the same material that makes up your hair and nails. Each scale has tiny ridges that act like **prisms**, breaking sunlight into the colors of a rainbow. The more ridges a scale has, the more colorfully the snake shines. Reticulated pythons are very shiny.

The scales on reticulated pythons have many ridges, so these snakes sparkle in sunlight. Reticulated and scrub pythons are the shiniest of the giant snakes.

Hunting by Heat

Giant snakes such as the reticulated python often hunt at night. Reticulated pythons can see very well, but they usually find their **prey** through their sense of smell and through special pits, or hollow places, along their lips and nostrils. Nerves in the pits sense the body heat of nearby **warm-blooded** prey, such as birds and mammals.

When hunting, the reticulated python moves its head back and forth. As it moves, it can measure the difference in temperature between the outside air and the body heat of its prey. The change in temperature helps it find the exact location of its prey. The snake then **lunges** to grab its meal!

At first, people thought the pits between a snake's nostrils and eyes might be extra nostrils or ears or places where tears drip. Now we know better!

A Squeeze to the Death

Monkeys are one kind of animal that reticulated pythons eat. When a reticulated python catches a monkey, backward-facing teeth in its mouth help to keep the monkey in place. Even if the monkey struggles to back out of the python's jaws of death, the needle-sharp teeth dig farther into its flesh.

The reticulated python quickly wraps its **coils** around the monkey, squeezing the animal tightly. When the monkey breathes out, the snake squeezes harder, pushing the monkey's lungs together. The monkey is unable to breathe and soon **suffocates**. The python then swallows it in one long gulp.

This reticulated python has already suffocated its prey. The snake is now swallowing the small rodent whole.

Prey for a Python

More than monkeys are on the menu for reticulated pythons. Lizards, birds, antelopes, jackals, sheep, goats, pigs, and chickens are all part of the reticulated python's diet.

Reticulated pythons may also feed on people. In some countries, families try to protect their pigs or chickens by bringing the animals into the house with them. Unfortunately, a python looking for a chicken for dinner may search a house and find a small sleeping child instead.

This reticulated python has a very thick body, even before it begins moving this pig down to its stomach.

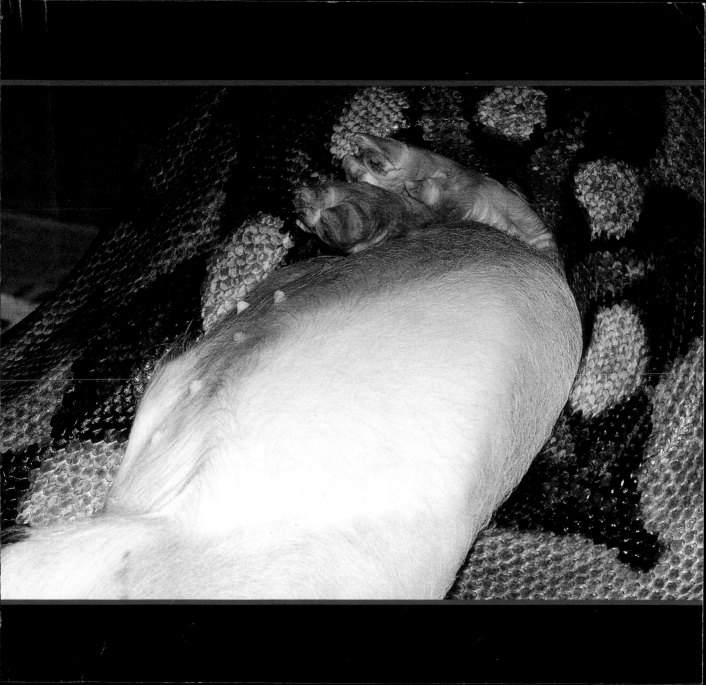

Protecting Eggs

Snakes have **evolved** from lizards. Some snakes have spurs — bony growths where legs once existed millions of years ago. Reticulated pythons use their spurs for **mating**, not walking. Males use them to tickle females to get them interested in mating.

About one hundred days after mating, a female reticulated python lays eggs. She sometimes lays as many as a hundred eggs. A female reticulated python does not simply glide away after laying her eggs. Instead, she wraps her body around the eggs, keeping them warm. She protects them day and night, and she only leaves the eggs to get a quick drink of water.

A mother reticulated python "sniffs" the air with her tongue, looking for danger to her eggs. Snakes and other animals might eat them.

The Egg Tooth

An egg from a reticulated python is about the size of a chicken egg, but it is not **brittle** like a chicken egg. Instead, it is leathery and flexible. Inside the egg curls a tiny baby python with a sharp "egg tooth" in its upper jaw. After about eighty days in the shell, the baby snake uses this sharp tooth to slit open the egg's tough covering. The tooth falls off soon after the python slithers from its shell.

Baby reticulated pythons are only 2 to 2.5 feet (0.6 to 0.8 m) long. They look like tiny versions of their parents. They can hunt like their parents, too. Without being taught by their parents, they can find and kill small prey.

It is hard to believe that this slim youngster could grow to be as long as a school bus! Snakes grow their entire lives.

Enemies All Around

Reticulated pythons are dangerous neighbors for many animals, but they also face danger themselves, from both animals and people. Animals that hunt in groups, such as wild pigs, may attack a python. Crocodiles will eat young pythons as they swim in streams and rivers.

People hunt reticulated pythons, too. Thousands of these snakes are killed each year for their skins. The skins are very popular for making shoes, boots, and handbags. Other pythons are taken live to be sold as pets, shown in zoos, or used in laboratories. People have built farms, roads, and cities on lands where reticulated pythons once lived and hunted, reducing the **habitats** of these fascinating creatures.

The reticulated python's beautiful skin makes it a tempting target for hunters. Some people are now trying to protect pythons.

MORE TO READ AND VIEW

Books (Nonfiction)
Fangs! (series). Eric Ethan (Gareth Stevens)
Pythons. Animal Kingdom (series). Julie Murray (Abdo & Daughters)
Pythons. Animals & the Environment (series). Mary Ann McDonald (Capstone Press)
Pythons. Naturebooks (series). Don Patton (Child's World)
Pythons. Really Wild Life of Snakes (series). Doug Wechsler (Rosen Publishing Group)
Pythons. Snakes (series). James E. Gerholdt (Checkerboard Library)
Pythons and Boas: Squeezing Snakes. Gloria G. Schlaepfer and Mary Lou Samuelson (Franklin Watts, Inc.)
Snakes Are Hunters. Patricia Lauber (Bt Bound)

Books (Fiction)
How Snake Got His Hiss. Marguerite W. Davol (Orchard Books)
I Need a Snake. Lynne Jonell (Putnam Publishing Group)
Snake Camp. George Edward Stanley (Golden Books)

Videos (Nonfiction)
Amazing Animals Video: Scary Animals. (Dorling Kindersley)
Fascinating World of Snakes. (Tapeworm)
Predators of the Wild: Snake. (Warner Studios)
Snakes: The Ultimate Guide. (Discovery Home Video)

PLACES TO WRITE AND VISIT

Here are three places to contact for more information:

Black Hills Reptile Gardens
P.O. Box 620
Rapid City, SD 57709
USA
1-800-355-0275
www.reptile-gardens.com

Oakland Zoo
9777 Golf Links Rd.
Oakland, CA 94605
USA
1-510-632-9525
www.oaklandzoo.org

Sedgwick County Zoo
5555 Zoo Boulevard
Wichita, KS 67212
USA
1-316-942-2217
www.scz.org

WEB SITES

Web sites change frequently, but we believe the following web sites are going to last. You can also use good search engines, such as **Yahooligans!** [**www.yahooligans.com**] or **Google** [**www.google.com**], to find more information about reticulated pythons. Here are some keywords to help you: *pythons, reptiles, reticulated pythons,* and *snakes.*

www.ecologyasia.com/Vertebrates/
reticulated_python.htm
Visit this page from the *Ecology Asia* web site to see photographs of a reticulated python. This python was found in a person's garden!

www.nature.ca/notebooks/english/
python.htm
Reticulated Python is from a web site called *Natural History Notebooks.* The size, habitat, and eating habits of the reticulated python are easy to find on this page.

www.scz.org/animals/p/rpython.html
Doing research on the reticulated python? Find information about the snake's size, shape, and weight on this page from the web site of the Sedgwick County Zoo in Wichita, Kansas.

www.xmission.com/~hoglezoo/reptiles/
retpython.htm
See a great photograph of a reticulated python! This page is from the web site of the Hogle Zoo in Salt Lake City, Utah.

GLOSSARY

You can find these words on the pages listed. Reading a word in a sentence helps you understand it even better.

brittle (BRIT-uhl) — very easily broken 18

cable (KAY-buhl) — a rope made of metal wires twisted together 6

coils (KOYLZ) — the circles a snake can form with its body 12

evolved (eeh-VAHLVD) — changed over a very long period of time to become better able to survive 16

habitats (HAB-uh-tatz) — places where an animal or plant lives and grows 20

lunges (LUNJ-iz) — moves forward in a very sudden way 10

mating (MAYT-eeng) — coming together to make babies 16

network (NET-wurk) — a collection of lines that cross each other 8

prey (PRAY) — animals that are hunted by other animals for food 10, 12, 18

prisms (PRIZ-uhmz) — pieces of clear glass or crystal that break up a ray of light into the colors of a rainbow 8

scales (SKAYLZ) — small, stiff plates that cover a snake's skin 8

scrubland (SKRUB-land) — an area of land that is covered with very short trees or bushes 4

suffocates (SUF-uh-kaytz) — dies from having no air to breathe 12

warm-blooded (WARM blud-id) — having blood that stays at the same temperature, even when the air temperature outside the body changes 10

INDEX